THE ESSENTIALS OF IKEBANA

SHUFUNOTOMO CO., LTD.
Tokyo, Japan

©Copyright in Japan 1978 by Shufunotomo Co., Ltd.

Seventh printing, 1987

Published by Shufunotomo Co., Ltd.
2-9, Kanda Surugadai, Chiyoda-ku Tokyo, 101 Japan

ISBN4-07-972482-9 C2077

Printed in Japan

CONTENTS

Color Plates

Preface

When Japan was opened to trade a hundred years ago and its "mysteries" revealed to the curious world, among the many arts that aroused surprised admiration was Ikebana. No one else had ever challenged the accepted standard that a rose on the right required another on the left, or that the best that could be done with flowers was to gather a rich profusion into a highly decorated vase.

Although asymmetrical design has now become a common practice, still when it comes to flowers, there are few who attempt it, and if they do, it is most likely to be a haphazard jumble. Guidelines are as important today as centuries ago when Ikebana masters realized that certain rules were necessary to bring out the beauty of the flowers and control the composition. As in any art, a classical form developed based on complex theories. But the fundamental principles are quite simple, and they are what all modern schools of Ikebana emphasize.

Knowing but a few of these guidelines, anyone with a love of beauty can create a pleasant arrangement that does justice to the flowers. That is the aim of this book: to provide the beginner with a concise, but dependable, foundation of essentials.

The essence of Ikebana can be summed up in the oft repeated precept "Flowers are cut, but not killed." No matter how the flower may be placed in the vase, there is no really "wrong" way so long as the soul of the flower has been captured and thus seems to be growing in perfect harmony with its new environment. Actually, the literal meaning of Ikebana is "living flowers," a far cry from the common translation, flower arrangement, that suggests the dominance of the human being manipulating the flowers.

A flowering branch is regarded with the heart of a poet: Is it lonely? Is it gay? Is it bent with age and harsh winds or delicate as a child's sweet smile? At the same time, it is seen with the eyes of an artist: the contrast of light and dark, of colors, of line and masses. Quite obviously, this requires an empathetic communication with the flower. Old Ikebana was so demanding in this respect that the person was even supposed to breathe in a certain way in order to achieve oneness while bending the branch or clipping the stem.

That the fundamentals of Ikebana had a religious origin is therefore not at all surprising. A Buddhist prelate of the 7th century Senmu is credited with establishing the basic principle that the arrangement should consist of three parts. Since he had in his youth visited China, it is probable that his idea derived from Confucian, as well as Buddhist and Japanese Shinto, thought since all respect the balance of the trinity and the triangle. Senmu also stated that there must be harmony between man and nature, which is the other main principle of Ikebana. The rest of his life was spent offering his flower arrangements, composed simply of three flowers, to the temple where he lived in a dwelling called Ikenobo, "the hut beside the pond." That is how the oldest school of Ikebana, Ikenobo, received its name.

Of course, this does not mean that flowers had not been appreciated before this time, nor that the only arrangements thereafter were religious. But Ikenobo brought a discipline to the joy of handling flowers, and it is this discipline that has made Ikebana unique in the world.

Remaining under the tutelage of artist priests, Ikenobo became the official word in Ikebana although later various other schools arose. From the first simple arrangements developed a formal style called Rikka, or "standing flowers." It was supposed to represent the mythical Mt. Meru, which itself symbolized the Buddhist universe. The highest point was the mountain peak, and there were to be a waterfall, a town, and hills. Some of the arrangements for palaces and mansions were enormous, and they are the predecessors of those now displayed in theater or hotel lobbies.

By the 16th century, Ikebana was a full-blown art with books of rules and plenty of theories. Flower arrangement parties and exhibits were held, and training in flowers was de rigueur for any aristocrat. Even the military ruler of Japan was taught by the famed aesthetician Sen-no-Rikyu. It was he who is said to have created the first Nageire arrangement one day when his student suggested that he show his imagination with some irises blooming before them in the garden. Sen-no-Rikyu nonchalently cut a few stalks, threw them into a wooden bucket, and produced a stunning masterpiece. The casual compositions of Nageire, "to throw in," became the popular alternative to the complex Rikka. Particularly as it was considered more appropriate for the feminine spirit than Rikka, every girl, every courtesan was expected to be proficient in Nageire or its stylized version, Shoka.

Shoka, or as it is sometimes called, Seika, was a clever compromise between the rules of Rikka and the presumed freedom of Nageire. Its main ideas were that there should be three branches rising from a single source and that they should curve in a graceful line toward heaven. Until the modern age, Shoka was the most popular style of Ikebana.

During the Edo Period (1603–1867), the policy of the feudal government was to suppress any revolt by controlling every aspect of life, including Ikebana. The schools became hereditary with a hierarchy resembling the government itself, and individuality was discouraged by adherence to rigid rules. However, the original creative spirit was quietly nurtured by a few intellectuals whose attempts came to be called the "literati style." When Japan was awoken to the modern age, there was a sudden rejection of anything old-fashioned. And then the literati style was in, its naturalism and self-expression greatly admired, even to the point of leaving spider webs on the branches.

Upon this foundation the modern schools of Ikebana were established. In 1910, a sculptor by the name of Ohara formed a school based on one of the original styles of Ikebana that had long been neglected: placing flowers in a low vase. This he termed Moribana. He had discovered that Moribana was the most effective way of arranging the many new flowers that had been introduced by the West. Indeed, it proved so popular that even such traditional schools as Ikenobo later incorporated it into their programs.

1930 was another turning point in the world of Ikebana. In that year, a group of Ikebana artists drew up a manifesto declaring that all rules, all conceptual theories, all botanical restrictions were to be rejected. "We must create a new image in a new age." Among these men was Sofu Teshigahara. The first to discover the beauty of dead branches and withered leaves, he also advocated taking flowers out of the vase if necessary to make them appear like a piece of sculpture. His Sogetsu School is now among the most important.

Although there are thousands of schools of Ikebana in existence today, they all fall more or less within the scope of the Ikenobo, Ohara, or Sogetsu styles, each of which represents an important period in the development of Ikebana. And each has a following of several million adherents, an indication of the enduring bond between mankind and flowers, or as stated by the present headmaster of the Ikenobo School, that "the life of man and the life of a flower are inseparable."

P.M.

7

Fundamentals

As we have seen, since its very beginning Ikebana has been based on the principle of three main parts, although sometimes two stems or in rare instances a solitary one makes up the arrangement. These are termed shin, soe, and hikae (or tai) in order of descending height. Here let's call them A, B, and C. Being the tallest, A sets the character of the composition. B, as an itermediary, supports A. C, always the shortest, by balancing A and B brings the arrangement to completion. These three main stems must all enhance each other in line, shape, color, and mood whether it be by contrast or homogeneity.

In general, two kinds of plants are used, with A and B or B and C of the same kind. However, excellent arrangements are also made with nothing but, say, chrysanthemums or roses. At other times, all three stems may be different, a more difficult arrangement to control as much variety can give an impression of disorder.

In order to recreate the vitality of growing plants, the stems are placed at varied angles, as well as at different heights. Seldom is there repetition except for the purposeful emphasis of some artistic aspect. Even when iris are placed standing in a row to portray their natural verticality, there are sure to be slight variations, for in nature no two things are exactly alike. Of course, this variety of height and line improves the arrangment which will thus be rendered interesting from several viewing angles.

The height of the three main stems in relation to each other and to the vase is of utmost importance for creating a harmonious composition. Each school has devised formulas for this as can be seen in the diagrams on the following pages. In the Ikenobo School, A is one and a half times the width of the vase plus the height, so a low vase 10 inches wide and two inches high would call for a stem 17 inches high. In the Ohara and Sogetsu schools, the height should be one and a half times the combined sum of the width and height of the vase, and therefore this stem would be 18 inches. Vases with other proportions produce greater differences, but they are relatively slight considering the fact that all schools admit freedom to overide these rules when the occassion demands. Following the set principles that Ikebana masters have discovered through much study and experience is the surest means of achieving an arrangement of balanced proportions and lines. However, imagination and an artistic sense are equally required.

So now let's see how all this is put into practice.

Measurement of (A), (B) and (C) stems

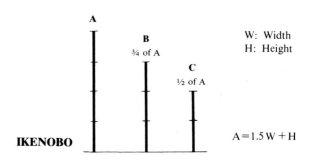

A

B
¾ of A

C
½ of A

W: Width
H: Height

IKENOBO

A = 1.5 W + H

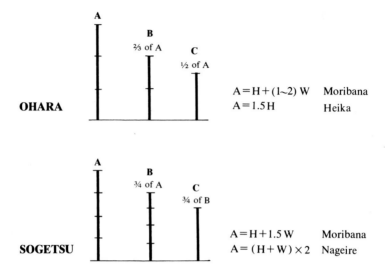

OHARA

A = H + (1~2) W   Moribana
A = 1.5 H   Heika

SOGETSU

A = H + 1.5 W   Moribana
A = (H + W) × 2   Nageire

"Erotic"

by Toshio Shoji   (School: Ohara)

Materials: Kentia palm, White cattleya
Container: Modern ceramic compote
Style: Moribana

11

"Tranquillity"

by Houn Ohara   (School: Ohara)

Material: Tree peony
Container: Chinese blue round container
Style: Moribana

"Dew"

by Sofu Teshigahara   (School: Sogetsu)

Materials: Dahlia, Caladium, Pampas grass
Container: Lacquered bowl
Style: Moribana—Free style

"Rhythmical Composition"

by Masahiro Ikeda   (School: Koryu Shohtoh-kai)

Materials: Loquat leaves, Marguerite, Aster savatieri
Container: Designer vase
Style: Upright parallel arrangement

"A Child's Heart"

by Yuchiku Fujiwara
   (School: Ikenobo)

Materials: Carnation, Pansy, Ivy,
            Camellia leaves
Container: Large shell
Style: Moribana—Oblique style

"Floating Flowers"

by Kohsa Moriya
   (School: Sogetsu)

Material: Water lily
Container: Glass plate
Style: Ukibana (Floating flowers)

"Beauty in a Decorative Design"

by Kasen Yoshimura   (School: Ryusei-ha)

Materials: Sunflower, Monstera leaves, Purple startice
Container: Two-tone (green and blue) glass vase
Style: Moribana

16

"An Emblem"

by Yuchiku Fujiwara   (School: Ikenobo)

Materials: Narcissus leaves, Tulip
Container: Ceramic vase
Style: Moribana—Oblique style

"Distracted by Love"

by Senei Ikenobo   (School: Ikenobo)

Materials: Cattail leaves, Vaccinium oldhami, Moonlight lily
Container: Ceramic compote
Style: Moribana

"Morning Dew"

by Houn Ohara   (School: Ohara)

Materials: Hollyhock, Hydrangea, Platain lily, Japanese pampas grass,
            Houttuynia cordata
Container: Sodeshi ware rectangular container
Style: Rimpa (In the mood of Rimpa style floral painting
        of the Edo Period.)

"Nandina"

by Houn Ohara　　　　(School: Ohara)

Materials: Nandina, Narcissus, Clubmoss
Container: White rectangular container
Style: Landscape arrangement
　　　　(Moribana style)

"Morimono"

by Toshio Shoji   (School: Ohara)

Materials: Grape cluster and leaves, Cosmos
Container: Reddish-brown carved wooden platter   Style: Morimono

by Houn Ohara

盛 花

*"Ikebana does not exist independently by itself but
as a link in the whole universe, each part of which is
endlesssly connected with another."*

(Sendensho 1536)

by Houn Ohara

by Houn Ohara

by Sofu Teshigahara

24

Moribana

Moribana, literally "piled up flowers," is an arrangement in a shallow vase. This container may be shaped like a dish, a flat tray, or a box, or it may be elevated on a base. The stems are inserted in a needle-point holder called a kenzan. Other necessary equipment: a pair of clippers, a bowl of water in which to cut the stems, and a cloth to wipe the vase and table upon completion.

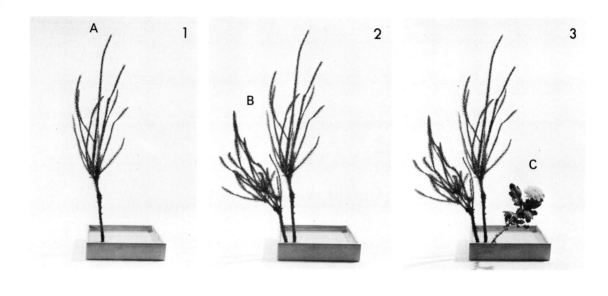

Upright Arrangement

First we shall make an arrangement with the tallest stem upright. Our materials are Japanese cedar and chrysanthemums. The A branch has been cut one and a half times the height plus width of the square vase. The B branch is three-fourths the height of A, and C, a flower, is three-fourths that of B.

First the A branch is inserted at the back of the kenzan in an upright position that is ever so slightly leaning off-center. This is to avoid the rigidity of a true vertical. The B branch is now placed to the front of A at a 45° slant. It is obvious in Fig. 2 that for the sake of balance C will have to be placed on the right, and as A and B are heavier than C, it should lean over further than either of them, in this case a 75° slant is chosen.

The outline is completed. Two more chrysanthemums of differing height, but shorter than the C flower, are added to fill out the middle and hide the bare stems. Termed fillers, they must never detract from the overall harmony of the arrangement, although since they are usually in the center, they may be the focal point as on page 27.

In this way the stems will be seen at varied slants on the frontal plane. Also viewed from the top, they appear fanned out at different angles. B branch is about 30° left of center and C, 45° to the right. All the stems lean forward to give the impression that they are reaching toward the sunlight.

It will be noticed that viewed from either the front or the top, the tips of the three main stems form an imaginary triangle. Training the eye to recognize the points that

Front view

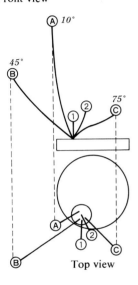

Ⓐ *10°*

45°
Ⓑ

Ⓒ *75°*
② ①

Top view

Ⓐ

① ②

Ⓑ   Ⓒ

1 Placement of (A) stem
2 Placement of (B) stem
3 Placement of (C) stem
4 Finished upright-style
   arrangement

hold the triangular framework will greatly fascilitate the choice of placement for the three main stems. By now it should be needless to say that the symmetry of an equilateral triangle should be avoided.

If the lay of the leaves and the flowers appears to better advantage on the right or to accommodate the setting for the arrangement, everything may be reversed. The kenzan may be placed at the front left or right, or as is often done in summer, at the back left or right to create a feeling of coolness by showing a large expanse of water.

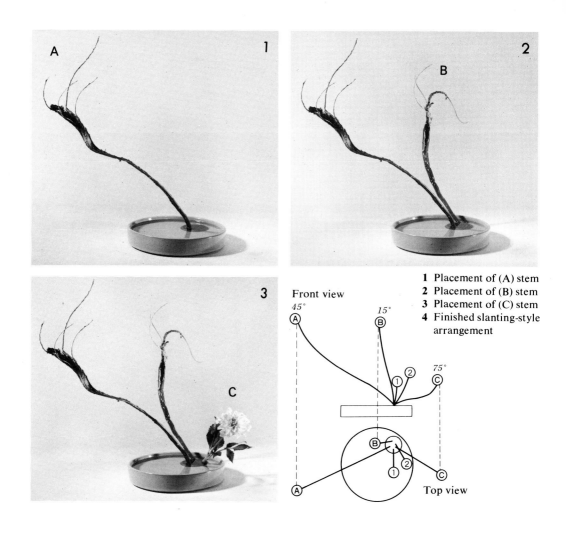

1 Placement of (A) stem
2 Placement of (B) stem
3 Placement of (C) stem
4 Finished slanting-style arrangement

Front view

45°

15°

75°

Top view

Slanting Arrangement

If the principal stem has a particularly interesting curve, it can be emphasized by placing it at a strong slant. In this case, the B stem is always placed behind it, rather than in front as in the previous upright arrangement.

Our materials this time are fasciated willow branches and chrysanthemums. The A branch is inserted at the front of the kenzan and allowed to extend at a 45° slant far beyond the edge of the vase. Since the kenzan has been moved to the right rear of the

container, the willow appears to be leaning over a pond. The kenzan may also be placed at the left front to create an even stronger diagonal movement.

In order not to interfere with the singular beauty of the principal branch, all other material is arranged to its right. The B branch has also been left silhouetted to preserve its unusual lines. In this kind of arrangement, B often is shortened to balance the strong outward thrust of the A branch. Notice that the curve of the branches and their twigs brings the eye back to the center of the arrangement. Also, because they reach upward, there is an expectant air of growth, of anticipation for spring.

This style produces successful results with any flowers that naturally incline such as lilies.

Cascading Arrangement

The beauty of plants that naturally bend downward or twine, such as willow or wisteria, is best displayed by allowing them to "cascade" over the edge of the vase. The basic placement of the materials is the same as for the slanting arrangement on the preceding pages; however, because the A stem usually reaches well below the base of the container, creating a most striking line, a vase with a high base is needed. Or, if you wish to use a low vase, it must be placed in such a way that the plant has room to dangle over the side, as at the edge of a table or shelf.

Here we have two clusters of grapes hanging from the A and B stems and one chrysanthemum. Great care is taken in the placement of these stems since even a slightly lower incline would make the whole arrangement seem to droop. No matter how a branch or flower is placed, it should always be imbued with vitality.

With the A stem resting at an angle of about 120°, B stem is placed behind it at a lesser slant, and C is almost upright to stabilize the composition. B is an unusual stem, having in effect two points of interest: the grapes and the terminal leaf which veers back in the opposite direction. To reveal the lines of the A and B stems, the components of such an arrangement are kept to the minimum. Here, no fillers were needed as the grape leaves are large.

C

3

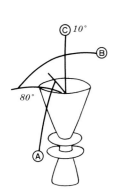

80°

1 Placement of (A) stem
2 Placement of (B) stem
3 Finished cascading-style
  arrangement

1 Placement of (A) stem
2 Placement of (B) stem
3 Placement of (C) stem

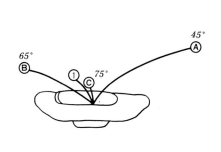

Contrasting Arrangement

So far, the B stem has always been placed in such a way that it echoed the line of the principal stem and the shortest stem balanced these two from the other side of the

4 Finished contrasting-style arrangement

arrangement. However, some plants take very effectively to what is called the contrasting style. In this case, the B stem leans in the opposite direction of the A stem, often crossing its base. The C stem is now in the middle. Being the most nearly symmetrical of Ikebana styles, it has an open, gracious air.

Our A and C stems are the bright red flowers of anthurium, and the B stem is the leaf. The kenzan is in the middle. As the A flower extends at 45° far to the right, the B stem is placed at a lower angle to the left. Both are slanted toward the front of the glass vase. The C flower, which has been kept very short, is directly in the center and projects forward. Note that the stamen points upward, as does the leaf, creating an imaginary arc that flows through the downward curve of the A flower. The balance of a composition is formed as much by the lines and their rhythm as by the length and placement of the materials.

It is usually necessary in this style to add a filler behind the C stem to help tie the opposing lines of A and B together. We have used one more leaf, a very short one, and have pointed it upward.

Vertical Arrangement

A vertical arrangement best portrays the stately grandeur of plants that grow tall and straight. Since all the stems reach toward the sky, the Ohara School terms it the heavenly style. To enhance their lofty direction, the materials are frequently longer than usual and the B and C stems are considerably shortened. In the arrangement on this page, the tall aspidistra leaf that serves as the A stem is slightly more than the conventional height of one and a half times the height plus width of the vase. The C flower, a carnation, is only one-third the height of A, instead of one-half.

The principal stem is placed directly in the middle of the vase. This leaf happens to have a natural curve, but if the carnation or an iris had been used instead, a perfect vertical would have been quite all right. The B stem is placed in front of A, slanted forward and to the left about 30°. The C flower is also brought forward at about 60°. One more very low carnation is inserted to the right as a filler.

Two filler leaves have been added just in front of A and cross over its stem to break the long line. All three leaves have been twisted at the tip, the top two forward and the lower one backward, softly repeating the curl of the carnation leaves—they, too, have probably been given a little prompting. These curling techniques and methods of bending branches will be discussed on page 48. Usually the shiny surface of the leaves faces frontwards as here.

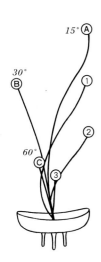

1 Placement of (A) stem
2 Placement of (B) stem
3 Placement of (C) stem
4 Finsihed tall vertical-style
 arrangement

4 Crysanthemum, carnation, and startice grouped to emphasize volume and color.

Mass Effect

The modern age has brought to Ikebana the concepts of individual expression and abstract design divorced from established rules. Shape, color, and line are often given priority over attempts to recreate or emphasize the natural characteristics of the plants. Since the flowers and plants are treated as art material, the foliage may be twisted, bent, or cut into geometric shapes. The flowers may be bunched together in clusters to serve as masses of color. Arrangements based on the rhythm of line are strikingly similar to calligraphy or abstract painting, and those interpreted according to volume, to sculpture.

Although it may seem that such compositions follow no rules, at least in the sense of

5 The three groups placed in a sculptural mass arrangement.

traditional principles, any good artistic work, whether it be in painting, sculpture, or Ikebana, will be found to somehow or other contain the universal art principles: harmony, proportion, balance, rhythm, and emphasis. Here it should be remembered that there is also harmony in discord and balance in asymetry.

In this example, white chrysanthemum, pink carnation, and sea lavender have been grouped into hilly mounds that play up the colors and textures of the flowers.

For mass arrangements, the flowers are tied together with string or wire beforehand and not inserted one by one into the kenzan.

1 Placement of (A) stem
2 Placement of (B) stem
3 Placement of (C) stem

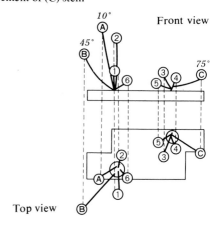

10°

Front view

45°

75°

Top view

Variations

Arrangement in Two Groups

Separating an arrangement into two groups gives a richness to the composition. The moribana theories discussed before apply here, too, the A and B stems usually being placed together on one side while the other group is centered around the C stem. This type of arrangement may also be formed with two vases instead of one.

A vase with a staggered outline such as this one pictured here is especially designed for a divided arrangement. The kenzan are placed one at the left front and the other at

4 Finished two group-style arrangement

the right rear. To avoid monotony, the two groups are never placed on a parallel line to the viewer.

Here we are following the principles of a basic upright arrangement. The A stem is placed at a slight slant into the left kenzan, and the B stem is put just in front of it, leaning at a 45 degree angle to the left front. Both flowers are large mums, a red one and a yellow one.

The C stem, a small white chrysanthemum, now goes on the other holder at a slant of 75 degrees to the right and a little toward the front. Fillers are added to both sides. Here two large mums and a small chrysanthemum balance the left arrangement, while one large mum and smaller chrysanthemums fill out the right hand side.

In general, the flowers in this type of arrangement are kept short and care is taken that the arrangement is neither overloaded nor too skimpy.

Front view

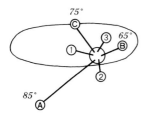

Rear view

Four Sided Arrangement

Whatever style of arrangement you may choose, it is important to consider the direction from which it is to be viewed. A vase in a corner needs to be arranged from only the front, but one against a wall will have a 180 degree viewing circle. Because they are seen from all sides, arrangements placed on a table are the most demanding.

The trick in a four sided arrangement is to spread the B and C stems in opposite directions from the A stem. Here A is placed slanting to the left front, B to the right rear, and C to the left rear. Three fillers of varying lengths are added. The material should be kept much shorter than usual.

Morimono

Appreciating the beauty of fruit and vegetables of the season is an enjoyment the Japanese have cultivated for centuries. Stylized arrangements are offered before the Buddhist altar, and at the moon-viewing season to the moon. In tea ceremony, a plate with one fruit or vegetable is passed among the guests to "feast the eyes." Since they are in reality plants, fruit, vegetables, or nuts certainly deserve a place in Ikebana also.

They may be grouped together or arranged with flowers as here and page 22. The principle of a main object with two subordinates supported by fillers remains the same.

1 Placement of (A) stem
2 Placement of (B) stem

Natural Scenery Arrangement

Another way of capturing the beauty of trees and flowers is to create miniature scenes from nature. Of course, these must not be exact reproductions of reality, but should be imbued with imagination and the person's own feelings for the plants.

In distant views, a branch would appear as a tree with flowers blossoming beneath it. The arrangement here is a close-up of water plants in the early autumn: arnndo donax, water lily (nuphar japonicum), and lotus.

A land arrangement is produced by placing tufts of club moss over and around the holder, giving the impression of a hillside. Even then part of the water is usually left visible as though it were a pond or stream. The two-group style is particularly effective for natural scenes.

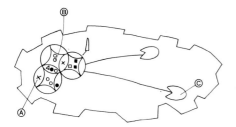 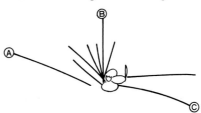

3 Placement of (C) stem
Finished arrangement showing water side view

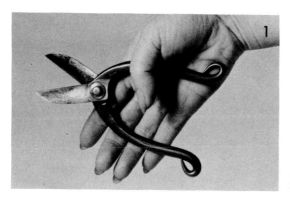

Helpful Hints for Moribana

Handling the Clippers:

Hold one handle firmly between the palm and thumb while manipulating the lower handle with the four fingers. Use the force of the whole hand when cutting. **(1)**

Thick branches are cut at the very back of the clippers. The tip is used for flower stems and for trimming off leaves. **(2 ~ 3)**

Successful Use of the Kenzan:

1. Branches up to the size of the little finger **(4 ~ 6)**
    1. Cut aslant.
    2. Push into the kenzan as far as it will go, then slant it to the opposite side of the cut.
2. Thick branches **(7 ~ 9)**
    1. Cut aslant on opposite side, or if very thick, cut part of the stem straight across and make several vertical incisions.

44

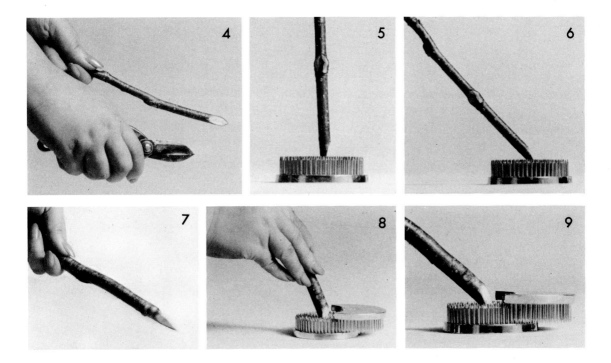

2. Insert the branch at the desired angle, taking care to push it to the very bottom of the kenzan.
The kenzan will probably have to be weighted down with another kenzan

3. Thin branches
   1. Cut aslant.
   2. Tie with wire to a cutting of the same material. **(10~11)**

4. Flower stems
   1. Cut straight across.
   2. Insert as wished.

5. Very thin stems **(12~13)**
   1. Very thin stems are wrapped in paper.
   2. Flowers that droop because they are too heavy for the stem to support are secured to a thick twig.
   3. Hollow stemmed flowers such as dahlias are pushed onto a twig that has been inserted at the desired angle in the kenzan.

Proper insertion of the plants into the kenzan cannot be over emphasized, and practice with the above methods will save many a disappointing failure. Decide on the position and angle of the stem before you insert it, because rearranging ruins the tip.

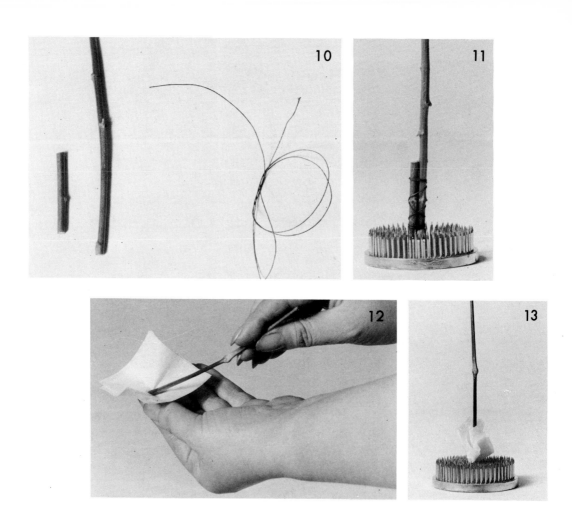

Shippo Holder

Some schools prefer the use of a metal "shippo" holder, shippo being the name of the pattern of interlocking circles. Although it may not seem as easy to work with as the kenzan, thin or succulent stems are held much better in the shippo. Besides, it is so pretty in itself that it hardly needs concealing.

A slanted branch is inserted into any of the openings so that it is braced against the walls. Vertical stems are supported by packing the space with short clippings of the same material.

1

2

3

4

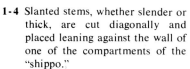

5

1-4 Slanted stems, whether slender or thick, are cut diagonally and placed leaning against the wall of one of the compartments of the "shippo."

5-7 (next page) To stand a stem vertically, the end is cut straight across and the compartment is stuffed with short clippings.

8-9 Thin leaves may be placed directly in the shippo but added support will hold them erect.

8

9

Curving a Stem

Branches and leaves are often purposely bent in order to enhance the line of an arrangement, emphasize the inherent curve of a stem, or make the stem fit better into the container.

1. **Narrow stems:** Grasping the stem with both hands, exert pressure with the thumbs and bend gently. Do this several times, also a little above and below the point you wish to curve. The stem and the hands should be wet. Stubborn branches can be coaxed by slightly twisting them while bending. This softens the wood fibers without fear of breaking the stem. **(1 ~2)**

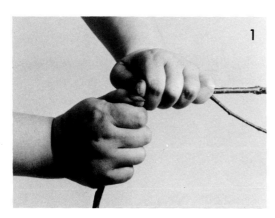

1

2

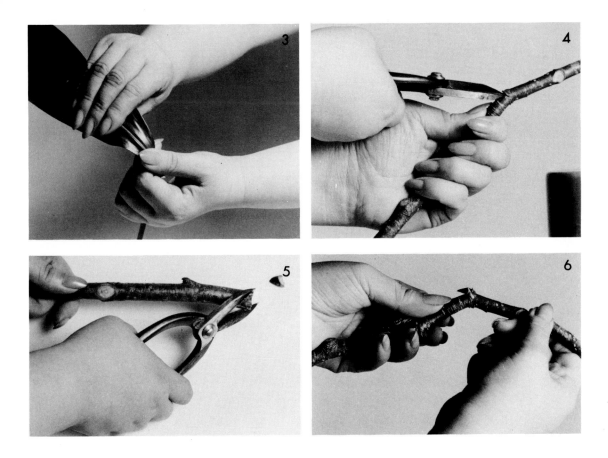

2. **Grasses and leaves:** Bend and twist as above. For leaves, though, it is good to maintain a hold on the base with one hand. **(3)**

3. **Thick branches:** Make a slanted incision about ⅓ through the branch at the point to be bent, and then bend it over the edge of a table. For a greater degree of curve, another cut or two is made an inch or so further down. If the branch does not keep the curve, a small triangular piece cut from the branch is wedged into the cut. **(4~6)**

Trimming

Do not be afraid to exercise judicious trimming of excess leaves, stems, and flowers. Trimming brings out the line of the stem and focuses attention on the points which deserve emphasis. As haiku poems have proven, brevity produces meaningful impact.

pomegranate

Chinese bellflower ——————————————————————— akebia ——————————

Note how the bellflowers have been rescued from the jumble of leaves this way. Trimming vines and fruited branches can be thought of in terms of a musical composition with smooth passages enlivening the active parts. Here the vine softly trails to an end that seems to continue invisibly into space; the pomegranate concludes with a strong boom.

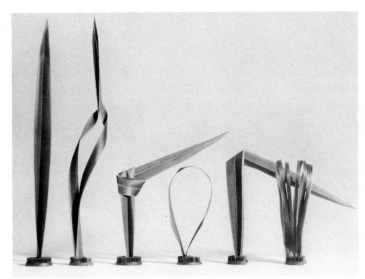

a aspidistra leaf

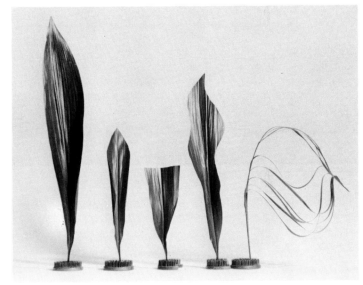

b New Zealand flax

Creativity

With the addition of the human imagination, a leaf can display new aspects of its leafy nature. For instance, tying young willow into a loose loop is one of the traditional decorations for the New Year season. Although this probably was first done to keep the long branches out of the way, it somehow is so gracefully willow-like. Here we see some of the sculptural qualities of aspidistra and New Zealand flax. **(a, b)**

How to Keep Flowers Fresh

The best time for collecting flowers and branches is in the early morning before they are touched by the sun; the next best time is at dusk. A cloudy day is more suitable than a sunny one. The cut flowers should be kept in plenty of water and in a dark place. Withered plants can usually be revived by sprinkling them liberally with water, then wrapping them in thoroughly dampened newspaper for about an hour.

The universal method for keeping plants fresh is to cut the stem under water so that no air may enter and water will be drawn up immediately. It is also important to change the vase water often. **(4)**

Here are some other methods which have been found helpful for certain plants.

1. Apply salt to the cut tip: summer flowers such as dahlias **(1)**
2. Pound the cut end and rub in alum: dahlias, wisteria, peonies **(2)**
3. Singe the end until it is black, then immediately dip in water: plants with hard stems such as peonies, hydrangeas, roses, thistles. Take care to protect the rest of the plant from the flame by wrapping it in a cloth. **(3)**
4. Dip the end in boiling water for two or three minutes: same as above.
5. After drying the end, dip in mint oil, vinegar, or alcohol for a few seconds: wild flowers, pampas grass, autumn branches **(5)**
6. Tobacco water or coffee or a combination of the two is pumped into water plants. Two cigarettes are soaked in a cup of water and the water is strained.
7. Thick branches are cut several times to enlarge the area of absorption. **(6)**

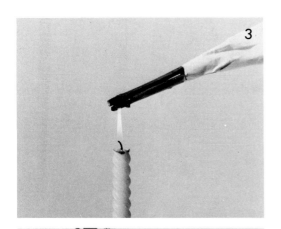

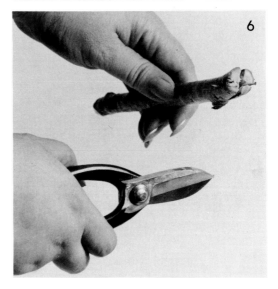

Flowers which Respond to Special Treatment

Amaranth: Boiling water or alcohol
Aster: alcohol
Azalea: singeing and alcohol
Bamboo: small bamboo—dip in vinegar
large stems—with a rod, pierce all
the nodes except the bottom one
and fill the stem completely with
salt water at a ratio of one teaspoon
per cup
Begonia: alchohol or salt
Bougainvillea: peppermint oil
Calacium: salt, alchohol, or vinegar
Calla lily: salt or alum
Chinese bellflower: Boiling water, singeing,
or salt
Cattail: ascetic acid diluted 200 times
Clematis: peppermint oil or salt
Cosmos: salt or boiling water
Croton: singeing and alcohol
Cockscomb: salt
Crocus: alcohol
Cyclamen: alcohol then hot water
Dahlia: boiling water, peppermint oil, or salt
Fennel: boiling water
Fuchsia: salt or singeing
Gardenia: alcohol
Gentian: alcohol
Geranium: mint oil, singeing
Hawthorn: alcohol

Hibiscus: alcohol
Honeysuckle: mint oil
Hydrangea: alcohol, boiling water, or singe-
ing
Jasmine: mint oil
Lilac: alcohol
Loosestrife: alcohol
Maple: salt, alcohol, or singeing
Morning glory: salt or mint oil
Nasturtium: salt
Orchid: alcohol
Pampas grass: alcohol or vinegar
Peony: singeing
Petunia: alcohol
Pink: alcohol
Poinsettia: alcohol or boiling water
Phlox: boiling salt water
Poppy: singeing and alcohol
Reed: vinegar
Rhododendron: alcohol
Rose: singeing
Salvia: singeing and alcohol
Snapdragon: mint oil
Stock: alcohol
Sunflower: alcohol or boiling water
Thistle: alcohol, mint oil, or boiling water
Verbena: alum
Wisteria: alcohol

"Dress Up"

by Sofu Teshigahara   (School: Sogetsu)

Materials: White lily magnolia, Scarlet rose
Container: Iwata glass flecked with gold foil
Style: Nageire—Free style

"Summer Breeze"

by Houn Ohara (School: Ohara)

Materials: Japanese pink lily, *tominoki*, Solomon's seal
Container: Chinese basket
Style: Nageire (Heika)

"Deep Valleys"

by Taiun Goshima   (School: Ohara)

Materials: Striped pampas grass, Stauntonia, Goldbanded lily
Container: Unglazed pottery
Style: Nageire—Cascading arrangement

"A Ballade of Midwinter"

by Houn Ohara   (School: Ohara)

Materials: Mandarin orange, White camellia
Container: Black glazed vase by Tamio Hibari
Style: Nageire (Heika)

"Mother and Child"

by Sofu Teshigahara   (School: Sogetsu)

Materials: Lilac, Narcissus
Containers: A set of Italian vases
Style: Nageire—Free style

"Starry Sky"

by Kasumi Teshigahara   (School: Sogetsu)

Materials: Clematis, Ivy
Container: Tall glass vase
Style: Nageire   Supports: None

"Light and Shadow"

by Sofu Teshigahara   (School: Sogetsu)

Material: White camellia
Container: French glass vase
Style: Nageire—Free style

"A Set of Two Single-Stalk Arrangements"

by Hakusen Umeda   (School: Ikkoryu)

Materials: Scarlet maple, Agapanthus
Containers: Round lacquered vase, antique Nambu vase
Style: Double-basic (vertical) style

by Houn Ohara

投入:瓶花

"The true student of Ikebana must also be a student of nature."
(Senei Ikenobo, XIVth Headmaster)

by Sofu Teshigahara

by Sofu Teshigahara

Nageire
or
Heika

Nageire or Heika is an arrangement in a tall, deep vase. These vases usually have a small mouth, but regardless of the size of the opening, the flowers are placed together in either the right or left front quarter of the container. Tall in this context means that the vase is higher than it is wide but not necessarily that it is large. A three inch high vase may be quite appropriate for miniature arrangements. The usual height, however, is around six to ten inches. There are also nageire vases that are to be hung on the wall or suspended from the ceiling.

As its name, "thrown in," suggests, nageire in its fundamental version made no special attempt at technical form so long as the flowers appeared perfectly natural in their new environment. Such an approach, because of its very purity, can be mastered only by intuition. However, this principle of freedom should be kept in mind no matter what type of arrangement you may choose. Nothing is worse than a forced composition.

For nageire, no kenzan or shippo is needed. Methods of securing the stems are shown on pages 78~83.

To ensure pleasing results, nageire can be approached through the same basic styles as moribana, i.e. upright, slanting, cascade, and contrasting arrangements. Again we have three main stems and their proportions remain, B three-fourths the height of A, and C three-fourths that of B. However, because nageire vases lend themselves to a stately, heaven-reaching mood, the A stem is two times the height-plus-diameter of the vase, instead of the usual one and a half standard of moribana. Often it is even taller. Also these measurements refer only to the portion of the stem that is seen above the vase. Therefore it is necessary to compensate for the amount that will be hidden inside. Fillers are used too, but they are kept to a minimum as the essential point of nageire is an airy informality.

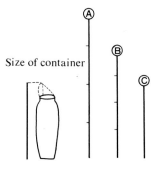

Size of container

Measurement of (A) and (C)
stems in Nageire

Upright Arrangement

Our materials are mountain ash and chrysanthemum. If you turn back to the photographs on the preceding page, you will notice that the main branch has been curved to create a gentle flowing line. It is placed at the left front, slanted forward about 15°. The rhythm created by the curve of the A branch is followed through by placing B just in front of it leaning forward about 45°. This left-right rhythm we will meet again in the classic style to be discussed later.

The arrangement is completed by inserting the C chrysanthemum so that it extends sharply to the right and then by filling out the area in the middle with two shorter chrysanthemums.

This leaves an open area embraced by the A and C stems. Although it may seem empty in the sense that there is no solid material in it, it is charged with a vitality that brings the lines and masses of the composition to life. Our eyes are too accustomed to seeing in terms of positive, concrete form; actually, however, the negative can be considered the more important because it defines the shape. With half-closed eyes concentrate on the areas surrounding this arrangement and you will see an entirely different pattern.

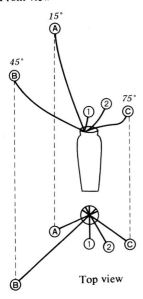

Front view

15°
Ⓐ

45°
Ⓑ

75°
Ⓒ

①②

Top view

Ⓐ

① ②

Ⓒ

Ⓑ

1 Placement of (A) stem
2 Placement of (B) stem
3 Placement of (C) stem
4 Finished upright-style
    arrangement

Slanting Arrangement

The light-hearted, spreading curve of chestnut branches is perfectly expressed with a slanting arrangement. The principal branch leans far over to the left. Placed behind it, the B branch sweeps upward after first paralleling the slant of the A branch. It leans about 15° forward. All the leaves below the chestnut burrs have been removed to show the curve of the branches.

Now, to the right we have a lily bud falling in a natural line toward the viewer. Two opened flowers, one in full bloom, unify the two sides.

Although the opened flowers have been placed in the middle, it is the bud that has the position of significance. Because a bud is full of potential, containing the unspent energy of the life force, it is stronger than a mature flower and therefore always is given greater importance. The progression of life is one of the beauties of nature that Ikebana attempts to describe.

4

15°
Ⓑ

0°
Ⓐ

Ⓒ *90°*

② ①

1 Placement of (A) stem
2 Placement of (B) stem
3 Placement of (C) stem
4 Finished slanting-style
arrangement

Cascading Arrangement

Angular and tortuous, pomegranate branches are silhouetted in fascinating lines when arranged in a cascading style. Removing most of the leaves has brought out their gnarled severity as well as the loneliness of the approaching autumn.

The A stem is bent down far over the side of the vase, and B is placed toward the back to give depth to the arrangement and to balance the weight of A. It begins with a leftward slant, but then sweeps over to the right. Notice that C, a Chinese bellflower, lifts its face up and toward the right, thus leading into the curve of the B branch. Also it is interesting that the fruit left on the B branch occurs about one-third along the stem and not at the end as on the A branch where it would have been too heavy. A clearly defined tip gives the impression that the line trails off indefinitely into space.

The materials have been shortened to accommodate this particular vase.

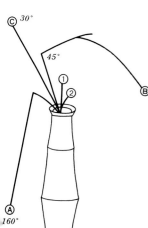

1 Placement of (A) stem
2 Placement of (B) stem
3 Placement of (C) stem
4 Finished cascading-style
   arrangement

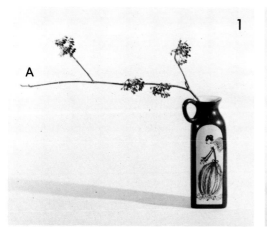

Contrasting Arrangement

Here we have a simple but effective combination of a cultivated flower, a carnation, with branches of seed-bearing mountain ash. The contrasting style of placing the two main stems in opposite directions works well for such spreading branches.

The A and B branches are crossed and both angled slightly toward the front so that they are not directly opposite each other. The stem of the C flower is placed in the middle of the vase but curved in such a way that the flower appears just off-center. It leans sharply toward the viewer. A second flower also rises from the middle, then arcs up over to the left, repeating the curves of the ash branches.

4

1 Placement of (A) stem
2 Placement of (B) stem
3 Placement of (C) stem
4 Finished strait-across-style
  arrangement

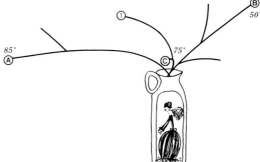

As important as it is to learn to recognize which materials and styles are compatible, it is also necessary to distinguish between the moribana and nageire. The anthurium we used for the moribana contrasting arrangement on page 32 would not at all be appropriate for the nageire vase, nor would the mountain ash be at home in the moribana style.

Double Arrangement

A double arrangement is different from a two-group arrangement in that each group is a complete entity in itself while working to maintain the balance of the whole. One group may be active and energetic; the other, quiet.

Contrast in types of material and color is also sought. The flowers may be placed in two separate nageire vases or one with two openings as here. If a nageire vase is combined with a moribana type low container, the contrast is further accentuated, giving much opportunity to exercise the imagination.

The dried grass of the taller group is tied in the tripod method. Although the A, B, and C stems are not distinctly recognizable in the mass of grass, they still invisibly hold the arrangement in shape. Six garbera of various lengths are placed in the lower vase, and they are given curves that swing in the opposite direction of the other group.

3

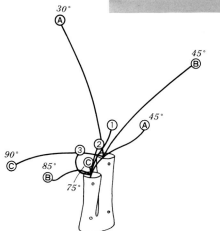

1 A handful of dried grass is tied at the bottom.
2 It is placed in the taller half of the double container, spreading the grass freely in all directions.
3 Six garberas of various lengths are put in the other half of the container. They draw the whole arrangement together.

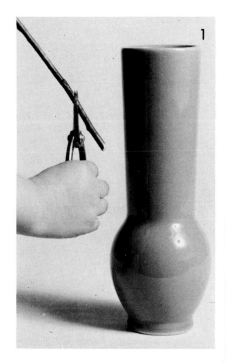

Helpful Hints for Nageire

Although the most direct method of nageire is just to place the flowers in the container, this is difficult with anything but narrow-necked vases. Large flowers are pulled down by their own weight and branches turn over. Several means of support have therefore been devised to solve this problem.

Light branches: (1~3)

Light branches often will stay in place by cutting the end at a slant corresponding to the angle of the wall of the container when the branch is resting in the desired position. The sharper the angle of the cut, the straighter the branch will stand.

Big branches: (1~5)

   If this is not sufficient, a prop is made. This may be either a vertical support as shown in Fig. 1 or a horizontal one that fits across the mouth of the container as in Fig. 4. The end of the branch is split and the support is inserted firmly in the forked end. Should the branch be unsteady, it is tied with string or wire. The branch can now be bent with the methods described on pages 48 to 49.

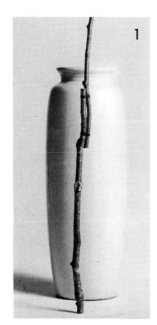

1

2

3

4

5

80

To hold branches upright: (1~5)

To hold a branch upright, a combination of the vertical and horizontal systems is employed. The side support is tied to the top or the foot of the vertical prop, which in this case is not split (Figs. 2 and 5.) The side support, of course, has to equal the diameter of the inside of the vase. When the mouth is smaller than the body, the side support is tilted as it is put in (Fig. 3.)

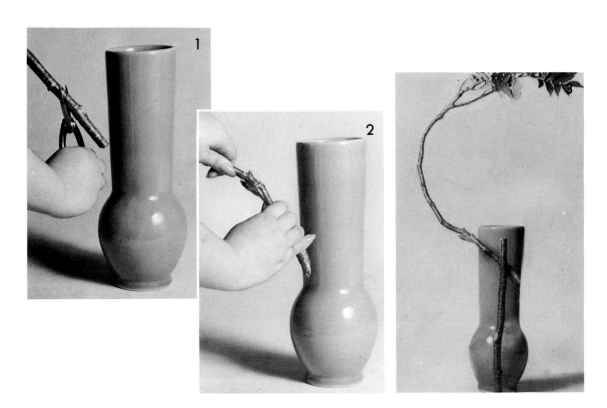

To hold curved branches: (1~4)

Branches curved upward are held by supporting the end against the inside of the container as well as by attaching them to a vertical support. The end must conform to the angle of the inside wall as explained above. Where the branch touches the rim of the vase, it is strongly bent or broken, then it is inserted into the vertical prop. Even greater stability is attained by constructing the support in such a way that the top end of the vertical prop also leans against the inside wall while the foot stands at the bottom edge.

Other methods: (1~3)

A quick, practical method is to wedge a single stick or two crossed sticks into the opening of the vase. The prop is cut slightly larger than the diameter. It is inserted at a slant and then the lower end is drawn upward until the stick is jammed fast. However, it is better to avoid this method for fragile or irregularly shaped containers.

For a glass vase, the tripod method avoids unsightly props, but it can be used only for wide-mouthed containers. After the stems have been placed together as they should appear in the vase, they are bound at a point just below the rim. The lower ends are then spread apart to form a tripod base as on page 76.

3

4

5

Although it is not recommendable for transparent containers, twisted wire is a simple and effective support. It may be placed just at the mouth or twisted into a mass that fits into the whole vase. Ikebana artists seldom use wire because they take pride in achieving a beautiful arrangement with as few supports as possible.**(4~5)**

Light material, such as grass, is held by bending the end of the stem and propping it against the inside wall of the container.

生　花

Classic Ikebana:
Shoka or Seika

As it has inherited the philosophy of Ikebana's religious beginnings, shoka stresses the spiritual nature of flowers and expresses their power to turn toward light and reach heavenward. Their growth being effected by external forces, however, all plants bend or slant depending on their various strengths and weaknesses. This has lent the characteristic curve to shoka. The main branch invariably sways to the right or left and then back again until the tip is at a point directly above the base. Sunlight is conceived as coming from behind the arrangement and off to one side. The A stem, therefore, at its base faces the sun, then gradually twists around until the tip is seen in profile.

The innate power of a plant and the forces exercised on it are seen in terms of *yo* and *in*, the postive and the negative. All things start out as one. Then the pull of *yo* and *in* begins to exert an imbalance which leads to growth. Thus in a shoka arrangement, all the stems rise from one source to later one by one veer off to left and right. When the two forces fall into harmony, they again become one, the whole arrangement focused at the tip of the main stem. In compositions with three parts (there is also a two-part style), *yo* and *in* have been likened to heaven and earth with man in-between. The stems are always of an uneven number.

Shoka is classified according to the degree of curve in the arrangement. Those that are formal and straight are called *shin*. Casually gentle lines are *so*, and between these two extremes is *gyo*. These can be sub-divided into the most formal of the formal: *shin-shin*; less formal: *shin-gyo*; and least formal: *shin-so*; and so on down to *so-so* which is the most informal of the informal.

The stem varies from one and a half to three times the height of the vase depending on weight and feel of the arrangement in relation to the container. B is usually ⅔ of A, and C is ⅔ of B.

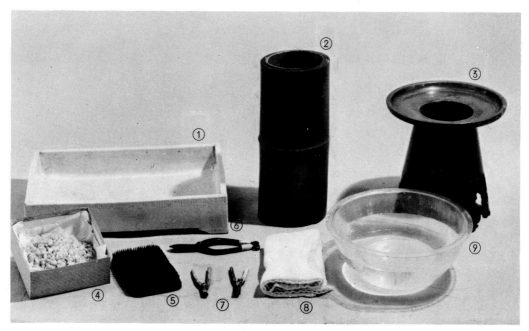

Equipment for Seika arrangement:

1–3 containers **4** pebbles **5** kenzan **6** scissors **7** crutches **8** cloth **9** plastic bowl

Top:
Shoka Style
by Senei Ikenobo

Left:
Small Rikka Style
by Yuchiku Fujiwara

Right:
Shoka Style
by Senei Ikenobo

"Iris Laevigata"

by Yuchiku Fujiwara   (School: Ikenobo)

Material: Iris laevigata
Container: White rectangular basin
Style: Shoka style—*Gyodo-ike* or fish path arrangement

"Niju-ike"

by Yuchiku Fujiwara   (School: Ikenobo)

Materials: Gladiolus, Phormium tenax leaves, Turkish broad bell-flower
Container: Bamboo with a double-opening
Style: Niju-ike—*So* style

"A Tsuki (moon) Arrangement"

by Yuchiku Fujiwara   (School: Ikenobo)

Materials: Laelio cattleya, Orchis graminifolia,
           Cymbidium leaves
Container: A full moon shaped vase of silver for
           suspended arrangements
Style: Shoka—*So-so* style

"Maiden"

by Senei Ikenobo   (School: Ikenobo)

Materials: Hanson's lily, Clematis, Eulalia
Container: Iron glazed compote
Style: Shoka style

"On a Summer Evening"

by Yuchiku Fujiwara   (School: Ikenobo)

Materials: Allium giganteum, Iris laevigata leaves, *Seiryubai*, Chinese peony,
                  Plantain lily leaves
Container: Pedestaled ceramic bottle with narrow mouth
Style: Small-Rikka style—*Gyakugatte-sugushin*

by Yuchiku Fujiwara
Rikka Style

Shin Style

The pure, straight lines of gladiolus set in a slender container display the highest degree of formality. Such deep containers are filled with pebbles or coarse sand on which a kenzan is placed. The base is covered with more pebbles when the arrangement is completed. A special Y-shaped prop called matagikubari may also be used, in which case only water is necessary.

Shoka arrangements are begun with the C stem which is placed with its sunlit, i.e. upper side or front, facing toward the back. In the case of iris leaves, this simply involves setting them into the vase as they grow and there is little difference from other styles of arrangement. However, if we were using aspidistra leaves, the moribana or nageire technique we have studied would have required them turned toward the viewer instead.

Next comes a filler complementing the A stem, followed by a barely discernible B filler. Now the A stem is inserted, and here the A and B stems happen to be together. A pin holds the material tight within the forked prop.

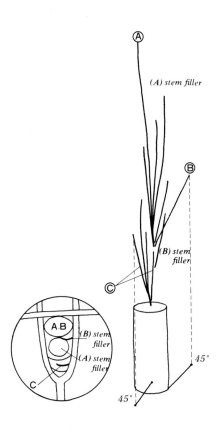

(A) stem filler

(B) stem filler

(A) stem filler

(B) stem filler

45°

45°

C

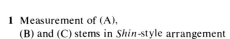

1 Measurement of (A),
(B) and (C) stems in *Shin*-style arrangement
2 (C) stem's placement
3 Fillers for (A) and (B) stems
4 Finished *Shin*-style arrangement

Gyo Style

In the *gyo* style not only does the arrangement have a greater curve, but the vase usually has a foot supporting a container with a large opening. The arrangement is filled out with more stems so it is not necessary to close the forked prop with a pin.

The C group made up of a cluster of chrysanthemums appears in the front. Then comes the A stem accompanied by two subsidaries directly in front and behind. At the rear is the B stem. All the material to either side and the back of the A stem face toward it.

To emphasize the upward thrust of plants, the stems are bare to a point about two inches above the water line. No leaf or flower ever is allowed to touch the rim, although the shortest leaf may bend slightly downward as it is nearest the water.

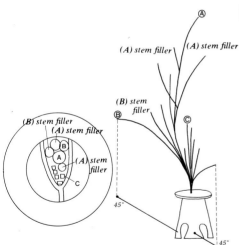

1 Measurement of (A), (B) and (C) stems in *Gyo*-style arrangement
2 Numbers indicate order in which branches are placed in the container.
3 6-filler for (A) stem placed in front of (A) 8-another filler for (A) stem placed at the back of (A).
4 Finished *Gyo*-style arrangement.

So Style

The relaxed atmosphere of the *so* style derives partly from the low, rectangular container that is similar to those used for moribana except that it is often slightly raised on small feet. Also as in moribana the A stem is the first to be inserted into the kenzan. Otherwise the shoka principles of the *shin* and *gyo* moods prevail.

The subsidary A stems are placed immediately next to A, followed by the C group in front and finally the B group in back. Figure 2 clearly illustrates the strong slant of the A stem as compared to the *shin* and *gyo* arrangements.

96

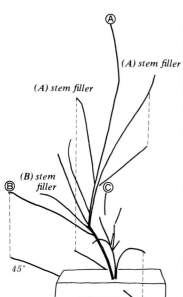

1 Measurement of (A), (B) and (C) stems in *So*-style
2 (A) stem and its filler
3 Placement of (A), (A) stem filler (C) and (C) stem filler.
4 Finished *So*-style arrangement

Ikebana Terminology

Cha-bana	Tea ceremony arrangement, originated by a master of tea ceremony. The beauty of simplicity is the main theme in this Ikebana.
Gyaku-gatte	Reversed way of arranging. Commonly, with the main stem at the center, the second stem extends to the left, but in this case it tends to the right.
Hana-dome	Holders, such as needle-point holder and metal holder called Shippo.
Heika	Synonym for Nageire. This term is used for a tall-vase arrangement in the Ohara School.
Kare-mono	Materials dried by natural or artificial methods.
Kenzan	Needle-point holder.
Kusamono	All kinds of grass material.
Matagikubari	Y-shaped prop.
Mizu-mono	Water plants or arrangement with water plants.
Moribana	Ikebana made in a flat vase and held in place with a holder.
Morimono	Arrangement of things other than flowers, such as fruit or vegetables.
Nageire	Ikebana made in a tall vase without any holder.
Rikka	Most classical style of flower arrangement, highly stylized and dictated by rigid rules and aesthetics.
Rimpa-Style	In the mood of the Rimpa School of floral painting which features grasses and a natural informality.
Seika	Classical Ikebana with detailed restrictions and rules. Also called Shoka in the Ikenobo School.
Shin, Gyo, So	Three classifications of Seika style arrangement. These classifications are each divided again into three groups.
Shin, Soe, Hikae	Terms for the three principal stems in the Sogetsu School corresponding respectively to the A, B, and C stems referred to in this book.
Shin, Soe, Tai	Terms for the three principal stems in the Ikenobo School corresponding respectively to the A, B, and C stems referred to in this book.
Shippo	Metal holder for a Moribana arrangement.
Shohin-bana	Small arrangement.
Shohin-Rikka	Small Rikka-style arrangement.
Shu, Fuku, Kyaku	Terms for the three principal stems in the Ohara corresponding respectively to the A, B, and C stems referred to in this book.
Shoka	General term for Ikebana, not to be confused with Shoka which is another term for Seika.
Suiban	Flat container usually used for Moribana, occasionally used for Seika.
Ten, Chi, Jin	Idea behind the Seika style arrangement, as well as the terms for the three principal stems: Ten (heaven), Chi (earth) and Jin (man).
Tsubo	Tall vase used for Nageire.

Ikebana Schools

Ikenobo; The oldest, the largest, and the most traditional of the Ikebana schools, it stresses the classic styles of Rikka and Shoka. Since the days of the founder, the head masters have been given the surname Sen. The present master is Sen-ei Ikenobo.

Ohara: Having revolutionized modern Ikebana with the introduction of Moribana, its only real rule is that one express one's feelings for the flower. However, it divides the types of arrangements into five styles: upright, slanting, cascade, heavenly, and contrasting. There are four methods to work with: color, mass-effect, line, and abstract design. The present headmaster is Houn Ohara.

Sogetsu: One of the most unorthodox of Ikebana schools, it believes the beauty of line is the richest element of Ikebana, the other being color. It classifies Ikebana into two styles: the objective which brings out the individuality of the flowers and the subjective which describes the person's feelings. Hiroshi Teshigahara, the son of the late founder, is the head of the school.